BEYOND EXPERIENCE:

The Path from Doing to Knowing to Wisdom

STEVE OLSON, EdD.

ISBN: 978-1-7381710-3-3
First Edition, February 2026

Published by Steve Olson Books
Calgary, AB

The information in this book is based on the author's personal experiences, research, and perspectives. While every effort has been made to ensure accuracy, the author and publisher assume no responsibility for errors or omissions, or for how readers choose to apply the concepts presented. This book is not intended as professional, legal, or financial advice.

Beyond Experience: The Path from Doing to Knowing to Wisdom is a work of nonfiction. Names, details, and identifying characteristics of certain individuals have been changed to protect privacy.

Cover & Interior design: Mo Keshavjee
Cover Photo: Kreem Elamawy (licensed)
Editing: Steve Olson, with suggestions from his reading committee
www.Steveolsonbooks.com   info@steveolsonbooks.com

DEDICATION

To Libby, who walks beside me;

to my children and grandchildren,
who remind me to keep learning;

and to Morrie, who proves daily
that wisdom sometimes has four legs and a tail.

And to all those still gathering experiences, still seeking
knowledge, and just beginning to weave the two into wisdom.

To Harold Olson, 1934-2025

ACKNOWLEDGEMENTS

Writing a book is rarely a solitary act, even when the words are your own. I owe deep thanks to the many people who, knowingly or unknowingly, helped bring Beyond Experience to life.

To my wife, Libby, for her patience, encouragement, and occasional reminders that the SodaStream cartridge doesn't magically change itself. And to Morrie, my four-legged field guide, for teaching me that slowing down and stopping to sniff everything is not laziness but wisdom in disguise.

I'm also grateful to my friends, colleagues, and former students whose conversations shaped many of the ideas in these pages. Your questions and challenges made the arguments sharper and the stories richer.

To Mo, who always seemed to be awake at 2 a.m. when I asked just one more question or needed yet another layer of design.

To Lisa, who keeps me honest about my motivation for writing and makes certain I never lose sight of who I'm writing for.

To Sabrina, for her valuable insights into the people and events that helped shape the foundation of this book.

To Michael Flynn, whom I've never met and who doesn't know I exist. While reading your novel *Eifelheim*, the idea for this book was just beginning to take shape. I felt a connection to your character Father Dietrich, who was wrestling with the same questions about experience that I was. Two of his Latin phrases ended up in this book.

And finally, a note of thanks to my unusual writing companion, ChatGPT by OpenAI, for providing structure when my thoughts were scattered, Latin translations when my high school memory faltered, and endless drafts when I asked for "just one more version."

The voice, ideas, and vision here are mine, but your coding DNA is stitched through the drafts. You also put my extended reading committee out of work. They thank you as well!

ADVANCE PRAISE FOR
BEYOND EXPERIENCE

"Beyond Experience *is a great reminder to anyone about how to get the best out of ourselves as we proceed through our careers and guide others in theirs. Great lessons and reminders of what we have learned versus what we know, and when balance between learning, knowledge and instinct is important.*"

A. de Groot

"Beyond Experience *brings abstract concepts of wisdom and experience into real life through entertaining storytelling. Steve Olson invites the leader/manager to reflect on the importance of both. Anyone in a leadership position will benefit from reflecting on the stories in this book looking both to their past, and into the future. Good learning and fun to read!*"

Darcy Smereka
Assistant Vice-President, Enrollment and Student Experience
St. Mary's University

ADVANCE PRAISE FOR
BEYOND EXPERIENCE

This thoughtful and grounding leadership book looks at experience, knowledge, and wisdom in a way that is both practical and deeply human. Olson brings his voice, shaped by years as a broadcaster, on-air personality and educator--literal and figurative voice-to his writing. It is insightful, generous, and encouraging. Carrying forward his mentoring work through writing is a gift and supports leaders at every stage.

Sandra Lee,
Executive director,
Decoda Literacy Solutions

"Beyond Experience *stands out for being a short, focused read that avoids filler and gets to the point. Its practical, down-to-earth approach is grounded in real-world examples, making it accessible and genuinely useful rather than theoretical or abstract. As a non-corporate leadership book, it feels refreshingly authentic, offering simple but meaningful nuggets of wisdom without being intimidating or pretentious. A real-world leadership book for the real-world situations of life.*"

Danny Covey,
Author

TABLE OF CONTENTS

INTRODUCTION

"Experience is often only shadow-work; wisdom is turning toward the light. Many lessons don't add up to understanding."

*—Plato; Heraclitus**

This book began with a simple moment. I was hiking with Morrie, my big brown dog, along a winding trail that climbed into hills that felt almost like mountains. We reached a bench overlooking a vast, shimmering lake. As we sat together, me holding his leash so he wouldn't bound after a chipmunk that was skirting along the side of a cliff, a realization came clear: **experience isn't the whole story**. To truly grow, we also need knowledge and reflection.

Not long before, my wife, Libby, had retired. Within weeks, we bought a fifth-wheel RV, hitched it up, and set out on a multi-year journey. We roamed through Southern Alberta,

---

*This quote is a fusion of two different sources. It is inspired by Plato's *Republic* (Book VII, 514a–520a) and Heraclitus, Fragment 40, *The Presocratic Philosophers* (Kirk, Raven, & Schofield, 1983).

up to Prince Rupert, through the Okanagan, in British Columbia, and spent the winter of 2024–25 in sunny Arizona. By spring, we were back in Canada and, as usual, chose a spot on the map we had never visited before.

The road to the campsite was narrow and winding. Cell service was unreliable, and I was ready to look for a spot big enough to turn our trailer around when we finally saw it: a forested park with a bright lake, green hills, and a dog beach that Morrie immediately claimed as his kingdom. We booked two nights, stayed four, and on day three, the regional supervisor strolled up and asked, *"Would you two like to be camp hosts?"*

It was an easy decision. We signed on as volunteer ambassadors with a few paid hours each week, performing light duties like site checks, wood splitting, and guest greetings. The work was simple, the pay covered our expenses, and the rest of the time we could fish, paddleboard, and enjoy the lake. No shirt. No tie. No dress pants. Yes, I wore shorts to work.

Within weeks, though, I noticed cracks in the way the park was run. Friendly people with leadership styles pulled straight from another era. Then came the conversation that crystallized it:

Me: *Where did you do your training?*

CEO: *What training? Growing up here taught me everything I needed to know.*

I've stumbled into this same trap myself, relying too heavily on experience without balancing it with learning or reflection. I've also seen it play out in media and education, when one pillar tries to hold up the whole structure.

Experience matters! It's something to be proud of. But it is only one part of the equation.

I once spoke with an executive I respect who told me she always scans résumés first for experience. Then she added, *"But I also need to see evidence that this person can adapt and learn."*

Her words echoed beyond the hiring process: they were really about life. To thrive, we need more than a history of doing; we need the capacity to learn and the courage to reflect.

Over the years, I've come to value three pillars: **experience, knowledge, and reflection.** Together, they create a foundation strong enough to hold wisdom; the kind that not only knows what works but also understands what's right.

Defining the Pillars

Here's how I use these terms:

- Experience: what we have done and lived through: the raw material of our days.

- Knowledge: the understanding we gain through education, study, or lessons learned from others.

- Reflection: the pause that turns experience and knowledge into meaning, asking, "What does this really teach me?"

Together, these pillars support something larger: **Wisdom – the capacity to act with perspective, discernment, and care.**

The Roadmap Ahead

This book isn't a textbook or a manual; it's a journey. It's a reflection on what I have seen, learned, and stumbled over. Think of it as a path we'll walk together, with stops, turns, and a few surprises along the way. We'll begin with the illusion that experience alone can make us wise, then test that assumption against the limits of the familiar. We'll pick up the missing lens of knowledge, stretch it through learning, and step into the uncomfortable spaces where wisdom begins to take shape.

Along the way, we'll see what happens when knowledge and experience collide, and how to hold steady between control and chaos. Finally, we'll bring the pillars together, apply them in real life, and consider what it means to leave wisdom as a legacy.

Experience

1. *The Mirage of Experience* — Why time served doesn't always translate into growth.

2. *The Limits of the Familiar* — How routines and traditions can lock us into narrow thinking.

Knowledge

3. *Knowledge as the Missing Lens* — Why fresh perspectives are essential.

4. *Expanding the Mind Through Structured Learning* — How intentional study stretches what we think we know

Reflection

5. *Wisdom Beyond the Comfort Zone* — The transformation that comes from risk and challenge.

6. *When Knowledge and Experience Collide* — Navigating the friction between habit and new information.

7. *The Space Between Control and Chaos* — Why balance and adaptability matter.

Integration & Legacy

8. *Completion of Wisdom* — Weaving experience, knowledge, and reflection into a whole.

9. *Applying Wisdom in the Real World* — Turning theory into decisions that last.

10. *From Wisdom to Legacy* — Passing wisdom forward with humility and curiosity.

Before we set out, I need to admit something. Friends who know me best have reminded me, and I've come to see it myself, that ego has often been my most significant stumbling block. At times, I've expected my degrees, my experience, or my credentials to do the heavy lifting: to earn respect, smooth the way, or prove I belonged. Instead, that posture sometimes created distance instead of connection.

Even the frustrations that nudged me toward writing this book, like my time as a camp host, carried that lesson. I wanted recognition; what I really needed was relationships.

This isn't a book written from a place of having conquered ego. It comes from wrestling with it, and from discovering – sometimes painfully – that wisdom doesn't come from proving yourself. It comes from humbling yourself enough to keep learning.

Who This Book Is For

This book is especially for those in the middle stretch of leadership: managers, educators, and professionals with hard-won experience but still flexible enough to grow. These are the years when decisions carry weight, teams look to you for direction, and the habits you form will shape the rest of your career.

If I had encountered a book like this in my 30s or 40s, when I was stepping into leadership roles in broadcasting and later in education, it might have given me language for what I was experiencing and saved me from repeating a few painful lessons.

That said, wisdom has no age limit. Leaders further along may find affirmation: a few "ah-ha" moments that clarify what they've developed intuitively. Some will find new terms for old truths, or a fresh perspective on what they've long known. And for those just starting out, this book can serve as a compass. It won't eliminate the need for experience, but it may shorten the path from doing to knowing to wisdom.

An Invitation

Wherever you find yourself on that journey, this book is an invitation: to pause, to reflect, and to see your work and your life through a wider lens.

Experience will always be where we start. But it should never be where we stop. So, let's take the road less travelled and discover the wisdom we can find.

CHAPTER 1

THE MIRAGE OF EXPERIENCE

*"Experience is a dear teacher, but fools will learn at
no other."*

— *Benjamin Franklin.**

This book begins with a problem: experience can be both a
great teacher and a terrible one. We value it highly; we list it
first on job applications, we seek it in mentors, and we use
it to justify decisions. But without reflection, challenge, and
adaptation, experience can stagnate. It can become a loop,
endlessly repeating while convincing us we are growing. This
chapter explores the danger of unexamined repetition, why it is
so easy to fall into, and how to recognize when experience has
stopped guiding you and started haunting you.

I've met people with thirty years of experience, and
people with one year of experience repeated thirty times.
Unfortunately, many in the second group think they are in

---

*https://libquotes.com/benjamin-franklin/quote/lbi1t2w

the first. Malcolm Gladwell popularized the idea that mastery takes 10,000 hours of practice, but I have never fully agreed with that blanket number. It depends on the skill, the context, and, most importantly, the quality of the practice. Thirty years in a role does not guarantee mastery if those years are spent on autopilot. Real growth comes from deliberate practice: focusing on improvement, seeking feedback, and making adjustments. Without that, "years of experience" often amount to the same year repeated, with no progress toward excellence.

That is the mirage. Longevity in a role may look impressive from a distance. It glitters on a résumé and sounds reassuring in a job interview. But up close, you sometimes find the same patterns, the same assumptions, the same mistakes, just lived again and again. As I will explore later in this book, meaningful experience is not measured in years alone. It comes from deliberate application, solving real problems, adapting to new situations, deepening understanding, improving decisions, and fostering personal growth. That is when and where experience truly shines.

One summer, I watched a regional supervisor run a meeting with no agenda, no objectives, and no real consideration for his staff's needs. Weeks earlier, employees had submitted feedback on organizational problems. Rather than meeting people individually to understand their perspectives and returning with a plan, he gathered everyone into a single large group. He arrived with two boxes of donuts and a cooler of drinks, declaring he "just wants everyone to get along."

This "food and goodwill" approach is a common trap in leadership. Tradition often disguises itself as effectiveness, and gestures of kindness can be mistaken for strategy. For a moment, the oohs and aahs over the donuts created the illusion of progress, but it quickly faded. The real issues remained untouched, and the room was no closer to resolution. The meeting devolved into name-calling and negative energy. By the time it ended, morale was not just unchanged: it was worse.

Wisdom in leadership requires more than goodwill or tradition; it demands listening, planning, and the courage to confront real issues directly. Without those, even the sweetest intentions can leave a sour aftertaste. What I've come to see is that when leaders rely solely on tradition or goodwill, they risk mistaking surface harmony for real progress. What looks complete may hide more profound truths, and those truths only emerge when we test our assumptions.

The danger of relying on tradition isn't limited to meetings. It reminded me of a lake I used to fish at. The regulations listed four species, but one day I caught a fifth that wasn't on the list. Later, I came across an old brochure that confirmed fifteen species lived in that lake. You can walk the shore of a lake for decades and still not know what happens beneath the surface.

Experience is not the villain here: it is often the first pillar we build. The danger comes when we mistake having done something for having learned from it. It's like assuming you know the whole lake just because you've walked its edge.

The same pattern shows up in leadership styles that lean on longevity rather than learning. I knew a manager with thirty years of industry experience. His leadership style was inherited from his boss, who had nearly forty years of experience. That boss's approach was rooted in early 20th-century "scientific management," a philosophy that treated workers like machine parts: valuable for their output, interchangeable, and expected to follow prescribed methods without question. It thrived in an era when repetitive, standardized tasks dominated industry and efficiency was king, but those same attitudes can suffocate modern workplaces that rely on adaptability and collaboration. In that worldview, a job well done was its own reward, and "no news" from a supervisor meant you were meeting expectations.

Imagine being a Millennial or Gen Z employee, raised in a culture of feedback and collaboration, only to be dropped into a workplace where "no news is good news" is the only management philosophy. The manager admitted he had never considered whether his team responded well to that style. I am neither a Millennial nor Gen Z. Even as a Boomer, I recognized that philosophy was already showing its age when I entered the workforce.

Too often, people manage as they were handled, or teach as they were taught, even when parts of that experience were unpleasant or ineffective. The unspoken reasoning? "Well, I turned out okay, so it couldn't have been that bad."

This tendency is what I call the **experience loop**: the repetition of unexamined methods, mistaking familiarity for wisdom. We'll revisit this in Chapter 7, where I explore how the loop shapes leadership and why breaking it matters.

There is an ancient idea, one we'll explore more fully later, that certainty only comes when a belief can survive its opposite without contradiction. Another says that it is experience that completes learning, not merely time spent doing a task. Both are worth keeping in mind when asking: Is your experience alive, or is it just echoing?

Pause and Reflect

- Think of an area where you have been doing something the same way for years.

- Is it still the best way, or just the familiar way?

- How do you keep your experience alive and evolving?

- How can you make your experience a guide instead of a ghost?

Experience alone is neither a hero nor a villain: it is a tool. But like any tool, it can dull through overuse without sharpening. When you repeat without questioning, you mistake comfort for competence and tradition for truth. What makes experience a hero is when it is joined with reflection, learning, and adaptation: the ability to challenge what you think you know, test it, and grow from the results. This book is about how to make that pairing happen.

The lesson here is simple: unexamined repetition can stunt growth. You might be tempted to think, "If it is not broken, do not fix it." But without examining it, you cannot know if it is truly unbroken, or if it is quietly holding you back from something far better. Recognizing the loop is the first step toward deciding whether it is truly working or just comfortable.

In the next chapter, I will look at how to test assumptions: to challenge the "truths" you have carried for years and see which ones hold up under scrutiny. Some beliefs collapse. Others endure and become the cornerstones of real wisdom.

> ## *Chapter Takeaway:*
>
> *Experience teaches, but it doesn't guarantee wisdom. Left untested, it can lock us into patterns that no longer fit the moment. Wisdom begins when we pause, reflect, and recognize that past success is not the same as future certainty.*

CHAPTER 2

WHEN EXPERIENCE FAILS THE TEST

"Experience is a poor guide, for tomorrow one may have a contrary experience."

— *Michael Flynn**

Experience is one of the most trusted guides we have, and one of the most deceptive. It shapes instincts, fuels decisions, and often becomes the bedrock of belief. But when experience is never tested, it breeds a quiet, dangerous certainty: the kind that feels solid underfoot until the ground shifts.

This chapter is about that kind of certainty: how it forms, why it misleads, and how to recognize when what is "known" is only true because it has never been proven wrong.

**Eifelheim, p.309.*

Evidentia potissima

"Only those propositions whose contrary reduces to a contradiction can be held with certainty."

Before you move on, take a moment. Think of one "truth" you hold because of personal experience. Could its opposite also be true in certain circumstances?

The more willing you are to ask that question, the closer you move toward wisdom.

Certain Without Breaking Logic

I once came across a Latin phrase that stopped me in my tracks: *Evidentia potissima* — "only those propositions whose contrary reduces to a contradiction can be held with certainty."

In plain terms, it means this: a statement can only be truly certain if its opposite cannot possibly be true without breaking logic.

Here is a simple example that passes the *evidentia potissima* test:

Water boils at 100 °C at sea level.

Argue the opposite — *Water does not boil at 100 °C at sea level* — and you collide with tested, repeatable science. This is knowledge verified through countless trials. It is rock solid.

Now here is one that does not pass:

The best way to train a dog is to use treats.

The opposite can also be true: *The best way to train a dog is not to use treats.* I know more than one stubborn, food-indifferent dog who would rather chase a tennis ball or sprawl in the sun than work for biscuits. The point? This "truth" might work in one setting, but it collapses the moment you step into another.

The Danger

That is the danger. Untested experience tempts us into thinking a method that worked before will work everywhere. We start making rules from patterns we have seen, forgetting to ask the more important question: Is this always true, or only true for me, here, and now?

I learned this lesson the hard way with Morrie. He was ten weeks old when I brought him home, and by the time the first snow fell, I thought we had it all figured out: house training complete, slippers intact, and, most importantly, a solid recall. He came every time I called, without fail. Confident, I gave him more freedom: longer leads, and even short moments off-leash in the fields near our home.

One snowy evening, Morrie bounded through the drifts, returning each time I called. Then a jackrabbit appeared at the edge of the field. Morrie froze, ears up, paw lifted, body quivering with instinct. The rabbit bolted. Morrie bolted. In an instant, months of training, and my certainty vanished. It took more than an hour to find him, and the only real lesson that night was how fast a big brown dog can run.

I couldn't be angry. He was doing what instinct told him to do. But I realized my "experience" of successful recall training was not enough: it hadn't been tested against the unexpected. The next day, I bought him an LED jacket. If he chased another rabbit at night, at least I'd still be able to see him.

That night with Morrie reminded me that success can look certain: until new conditions test it.

Buckets and Toboggans

I grew up on a farm where winter taught me another version of the same lesson. In summer, watering cattle was simple: run a hose from the well pump to the trough. Winter was different. The hose froze, and I was left hauling one five-gallon pail at a time. Fifteen exhausting trips.

Then I discovered our old toboggans. The small metal one carried a single bucket with ease. The larger wooden one carried three. Five trips instead of fifteen. Tradition said, "carry the bucket," but reflection showed a better way.

Sometimes you have to step back to see that effort and tradition aren't the same as wisdom.

Expensive Guesswork

I ran into that lesson again early in my radio career. The general manager handed me a reel-to-reel master tape of a live performance and asked me to edit it down to thirty minutes for broadcast. The problem? I had never edited tape in my life. I didn't say that out loud. I didn't want to look unqualified, and I assumed I could figure it out.

Armed with scissors, Scotch tape, and misplaced confidence, I hacked through hours of music. The tape stuck, my edits jumped off-beat, and because I didn't know the difference between the playback and record heads, every splice was about an inch off. The result was unlistenable. Worse, I had done it all on the master tape: the one thing I should never have touched. The program never aired.

What saved me was finally admitting defeat and asking the production manager to show me how to splice tape properly. It was a humbling moment and a reminder that experience without knowledge is just guesswork. Sometimes, expensive guesswork.

Whether it's a runaway dog, frozen buckets, or tangled audio tape, the point is the same: experience alone is never enough. Without knowledge and reflection, it can leave you chasing, straining, or splicing the wrong thing entirely.

Individuals and Nations

Nations fall into the same trap. France built the Maginot Line:* brilliant for the last war, but useless in the next.

That same mistake repeats itself in organizations today. I've seen teams made up of multiple generations – retirees working alongside those at the beginning of their careers, with mid-career staff in between – all managed as though they needed the same things.

Equal treatment is not the same as giving people what they need to thrive. Leaders who assume otherwise are leaning on untested tradition, much like France leaned on the Maginot Line. Without adapting to the realities of today's workforce, certainty can crumble the moment it's tested: a philosophy that would never pass the *evidentia potissima* test.

The Maginot Line was a line of defensive fortifications built by France along its eastern border in the 1930s, intended to deter a German invasion. During World War II, German forces bypassed it in 1940 by invading through Belgium, rendering the costly fortifications largely ineffective.

Getting Closer to Wisdom

Evidentia potissima is a reminder to pause before declaring certainty. Experience alone cannot tell us what is true in every circumstance. But when it is paired with tested knowledge, we begin to build something closer to wisdom.

So pause and ask: How much of what you "know" is only true because you have never personally seen it proven wrong?

In my years working with leaders, I have met many who built their approach entirely on personal history. If they had not been burned by something before, they assumed it was safe. If a tactic had worked once, they treated it as law. Without testing those beliefs, they risked leading with misplaced certainty.

Experience, no matter how deep, is only a starting point. Without the reinforcement of reflection and tested knowledge, it is just a sandbar: stable until the tide rises. The leaders who endure are those willing to test their certainties before reality tests them in harsher ways.

If experience isn't enough, what is? The next chapter turns to knowledge: the lens that can sharpen, correct, and expand what our experience only hints at.

Chapter Takeaway:

Confidence without testing is a dangerous illusion. Experience may feel reliable, but the moment conditions change it can collapse without warning. True wisdom comes from challenging even our most familiar lessons to see if they still hold.

CHAPTER 3

KNOWLEDGE AS THE MISSING LENS

"An investment in knowledge pays the best interest."
— *Benjamin Franklin**

How many of your most confident decisions have never truly been tested?

If Chapter 2 was about the danger of untested experience, this chapter is about the next step: putting what we "know" under pressure to see if it holds.

Untested Beliefs

Every belief we carry has a history. Some are built from personal victories, some from hard lessons, and some from ideas we absorbed without noticing. The danger is not in having beliefs, but in leaving them unchallenged. An untested belief can feel as solid as granite yet crumble the moment it meets a different perspective or a changing reality.

---

*https://www.brainyquote.com/quotes/benjamin_franklin_141119

Testing what we think we know isn't about cynicism or tearing down every idea. It's about building confidence in the beliefs that survive examination. The process often exposes ideas that were true once but no longer match the world we live in. It also strengthens the beliefs that prove resilient, turning them into something more than habit or inherited wisdom.

My wife, Libby, once worked at a large shelter for people experiencing homelessness. There, she discovered an unwritten rule: making an exception for one client was frowned upon. The logic was simple: if you do it for one, you must do it for everyone.

This rule wasn't in a policy manual. It grew from repeated conflicts where unequal treatment led to complaints. Over time, those incidents hardened into a guiding principle: exceptions are dangerous.

But the belief wasn't always true. Sometimes, a small act of flexibility, what others might call bending a rule, was exactly what someone needed to move forward.

Clients often left the shelter at 5:30 a.m. for day-labour sites. That early start meant many missed breakfast. If they picked up work, they'd be gone all day, surviving on perhaps a sandwich and a granola bar if any were available. By the time they returned, sometimes half an hour or more after dinner service had ended, no client meals remained. The unwritten rule was clear: if you missed dinner, you missed dinner.

Libby often broke that rule. Sometimes she would find a leftover staff meal. More often, she gave them food I had packed for her dinner. Our philosophy was simple: if I sent her with a meal, that left one more portion available for someone who needed it. She knew that nourishment could give someone the strength to return the next morning: a slight push toward building positive cycles. (I should add, my homemade beef and barley soup became something of a hit. Libby loved offering that little touch of "home" to a client.)

Her small acts of kindness were labelled 'exceptions,' but they were really wisdom in practice. Libby wasn't rebelling against the organization; she was honouring the deeper intent of its mission: to sustain people. And her choices didn't just impact the clients. Over time, other staff quietly followed her example, giving up their own meals so someone else could eat. For many clients, that meal was the only one they would have that day.

It was a reminder that experience may set the rule, but only reflection reveals when wisdom asks us to bend it.

Pause and Reflect

Think of a "rule" in your workplace, family, or community that everyone follows without question. Where did it come from? Was it born from repeated experience, or backed by tested knowledge? Now ask yourself: could the opposite also be true in certain situations? Wisdom often begins with the courage to revisit old rules.

The Kidney Scenario

From the small scale of a shelter meal to the moral weight of life-and-death choices, the pattern is the same: rules often collapse or transform when tested.

Several years ago, I was teaching an introductory leadership course to IT professionals. One of the group exercises was designed to spark a complex debate. Participants received a list of twenty people: some famous, like Oprah Winfrey or Bill Gates, others anonymous, like a 14-year-old girl or a teenager in a wheelchair.

The scenario was stark: all twenty needed a life-saving kidney transplant. Only a few kidneys were available, perhaps two, maybe four. Each group had to decide who would receive them.

In most years, groups spent the entire time debating merits: youth versus age, past contributions versus future potential. The discussions were spirited and often emotional, but always focused on prioritizing lives by perceived value.

One year, however, a group finished in just minutes. When presenting to the class, their spokesperson said, "We decided to put all the names in a hat and draw them at random."

I was stunned. This had never happened before. It challenged the unspoken assumption behind the exercise.

Rather than reject their answer, I asked them to explain. They pointed to a classmate named Nicolas. He spoke quietly: before moving to Canada for school, he had served in the military in Eastern Europe. He had aimed at "the enemy" through a rifle scope and pulled the trigger. "When it came to this exercise," he said, "I didn't want to play God anymore."

The room fell silent. A few students were in tears. I shifted the discussion, asking the class to reflect on the impossible decisions leaders sometimes face, and how Nicolas' choice might change their approach.

That day, I learned something important: sometimes the value of an exercise isn't in confirming the lesson you planned, but in recognizing the lesson the room needs. From then on, I shared Nicolas' story with future groups, then asked them:

- How does this change the exercise for you?

- And later: How will you respond when an employer asks you to do something you believe is ethically wrong?

That moment reminded me that experience may set the stage, and knowledge may shape the exercise, but only reflection reveals the more profound wisdom waiting in the room.

Four Ways to Stress-Test a Belief

1. Reverse the Assumption

Ask, *"What if the opposite were true?"*

If you believe "personal attention creates problems," imagine a scenario where it creates solutions. What conditions would make that possible? This reframing often reveals hidden exceptions.

2. Change the Conditions

Test the belief outside the context in which it formed.

A practice that works in a small team may fail in a larger organization — or vice versa. Altering the scale, timing, environment, or participants can expose weaknesses or confirm resilience.

3. Seek the Outsider's View

Invite someone without your history or stake in the matter to challenge the belief.

Fresh perspectives can spot blind spots and inherited habits you've stopped questioning.

4. Simulate the Worst Case

Ask, *"If this belief is wrong, what could it cost us?"*

Run thought experiments, small-scale pilots, or "pre-mortems" to explore potential failure points before reality does the testing for you.

Greater Consequences

My own experience was in a classroom. In other settings, the consequences of untested assumptions have been far greater.

In 1986, NASA's Challenger disaster revealed the cost of trusting a pattern without re-examining it. Engineers had launched shuttles many times before and seen minor O-ring erosion without catastrophic results. Experience told them the design was sound. That is, until a cold January morning exposed the flaw. The O-rings, brittle from the temperature, failed, and tragedy followed.

The lesson is brutal but clear: repeated success in the same conditions doesn't mean a system is safe in all conditions.

And yet, testing can also turn an unproven belief into an unshakable truth. In 1954, Dr. Jonas Salk had promising early results for his polio vaccine. Some urged an immediate rollout. But Salk insisted on one of the most extensive medical trials in history, involving over a million children. The results didn't just confirm his belief; they cemented it as a global consensus.

Experience may give us confidence, but only testing gives us certainty. When we challenge what we "know," we either uncover a weakness or confirm a truth: both outcomes leave us stronger.

The real danger is not in being wrong, but in never finding out. Knowledge that is never tested is only opinion. Knowledge that survives the test becomes the foundation.

Bottom Line

In the next chapter, we'll explore how to build environments where assumptions can be challenged without damaging morale; where beliefs that endure testing emerge sharper, stronger, and ready for whatever the future throws at them.

Chapter Takeaway:

Experience may give us confidence, but only testing gives us certainty. When we put our beliefs under pressure, we either uncover a weakness or confirm a truth: both outcomes make us stronger. The danger isn't in being wrong: it's never finding out.

CHAPTER 4

EXPANDING THE MIND THROUGH STRUCTURED LEARNING

"One's mind, once stretched by a new idea, never regains its original dimensions."

— *Oliver Wendell Holmes**

Henry Ford never earned a degree. The Wright brothers never studied engineering. Yet they reshaped entire industries. What they shared wasn't credentials but curiosity, experimentation, and reflection: a kind of "structured learning" of their own. Structured learning doesn't just mean a diploma; it can take many forms: classrooms, mentors, or disciplined self-study. The point is simple: experience stalls at competence unless it is tested and expanded.

---

*https://philosiblog.com/2012/08/30/ones-mind-once-stretched-by-a-new-idea-never-regains-its-original-dimensions/

The Worst Writer in the Room

Three days after graduating high school, I landed my first radio job. A few months later, my general manager looked me straight in the eye and told me I might be the worst writer he'd seen in decades. He wasn't exaggerating. I had barely passed high school English, and my scripts showed it.

The small town where I worked offered short courses through an extension program: résumé writing, basic accounting, and balancing a cheque book. One course stood out: Foundations of Writing.

Much of it went over my head at the time, but one lesson stuck: review your writing from the reader's perspective. Reading my work aloud, something natural for a radio announcer, instantly revealed awkward phrasing and unclear ideas.

From that point on, I read everything aloud. Over the years, my ear has improved to the point where I no longer need to do it every time, but the habit still surfaces. It wasn't a degree, but that short course gave me a tool I still use decades later. Structured learning doesn't just sharpen skills; sometimes it changes the trajectory of your life.

A Redirected Dream

Seven years after high school, I had the chance to attend post-secondary school. By then, I'd taught myself BASIC programming and had already written software for the radio station, including one program that calculated the annual Top 100 countdown in hours instead of days.

When I later learned my "brilliant" sorting method was wildly inefficient, it didn't matter. At the time, it felt like magic. My Program Director encouraged me to pursue a credential to strengthen my career. Naturally, I thought of computer science.

That plan ended quickly. The University of Calgary required advanced math and calculus, neither of which I had. Math and I have always maintained a respectful but distant relationship.

Seeing my disappointment, Libby suggested I study my favourite subject instead. For me, that was drama. I shifted my focus, enrolled in a Bachelor of Fine Arts program, and eventually earned a Master's in Theatre History.

At the time, it felt like abandoning one dream. In hindsight, it was a redirection: one that kept my creativity alive, sharpened my storytelling, and shaped the teaching and leadership I later brought to broadcasting and education. Structured learning doesn't just prepare us for the paths we expect; it equips us for paths we never imagined.

What a Degree Really Signals

When I began teaching at the Southern Alberta Institute of Technology (SAIT), I brought over twenty years of broadcasting experience. No formal training in radio, just lived experience and two theatre degrees that, on paper, had little to do with broadcasting.

The Dean who hired me wasn't concerned about the subject matter of my degrees. What mattered was that I had earned a master's degree. At first, I bristled: two decades in radio felt like my strongest qualification. Experience was the first thing I listed on the job application!

Over time, I came to see the lesson: in many settings, a degree isn't about the subject itself. It's shorthand for persistence, discipline, and the ability to take on complex work and see it through.

Education at Any Age

If you want to take a course, earn a certificate, or pursue a credential: do it. Age is irrelevant.

Paths of Structured Learning — and What They Offer

1. Academic Degrees

Pros: Comprehensive, recognized, develops broad intellectual skills.

Cons: Time-consuming, expensive, may include unrelated requirements.

2. Professional Certifications

Pros: Industry-specific, targeted, often faster to complete.

Cons: Narrow focus, may need frequent renewal.

3. Workshops and Short Courses

Pros: Flexible, immediately applicable, low cost.

Cons: Limited depth, requires follow-up to sustain learning.

4. Mentorship and Apprenticeship Programs

Pros: Practical, relationship-based, context-specific.

Cons: Dependent on mentor quality, limited exposure to outside perspectives.

When I started my BFA, I was in my mid-twenties. The oldest student in my class was 87, chasing a lifelong dream to act. Watching her graduate was pure joy.

When I returned to school for my Doctorate in Education at age 50, my cohort ranged from their mid-thirties to their seventies. At orientation, the Vice President Academic gave the familiar "look to your left, look to your right" speech, warning that two-thirds of us wouldn't finish unless we gave 100% to the program.

Instead of 'how bad do you want it,' I found better results when I answered the question: *What do you want, and what are you willing to give up to get it?*

Here is my rule:

- Some things in life are non-negotiable: work, weekly date night with Libby, Sunday family dinners, and one night a week playing World of Warcraft with my sons.
- Other things are negotiable: movies, casual reading, and most video games. Those became study time.

That approach, combined with a strong support system and a bit of discipline, has seen me through many large projects. The real success isn't just finishing; it is proving that education can fit into the life you value instead of replacing it.

NON-NEGOTIABLE vs. NEGOTIABLE

List your firm commitments and flexible activities to create a sustainable plan for education.

Non-Negotiable	Negotiable
• Work	• Casual reading
• Date Night	• Movies
• Sunday Dinner with Family	• Video Games

The Core Lesson

Formal learning and experience don't compete; they complete each other.

One proves you can do; the other proves you can learn. Together, they give you confidence and adaptability: the ability to handle familiar challenges and navigate uncharted territory.

If experience gives you a map, structured learning adds new continents. Once you've seen them, you can't return to the smaller world you started with. Holmes was right: a mind stretched by a new idea never regains its original dimensions.

The choice to keep learning, whether through a weekend workshop or a doctorate, is more than a career move. It's a refusal to stagnate. It's how you stay relevant in a changing world and ensure your skills evolve alongside your experience.

Pause and Reflect

- Have you ever had a career or education plan blocked by a requirement you didn't meet?

- Did you push through, find a workaround, or choose another path?

- Looking back, did that detour limit you, or lead to unexpected growth?

- Is there a subject you've always wanted to study, regardless of its 'practical' value? What might pursuing it add to your life?

One Final Insight

In more than twenty-five years working in post-secondary education, I've noticed something consistent: students who choose subjects they're passionate about tend to be more engaged, and engaged learners succeed more often.

Sometimes you need a credential to advance in your field. But more often, it's the act of completing the credential itself – proving you can persist and finish – that opens doors. So, if you're stuck deciding what education to pursue, choose the subject that excites you. Passion fuels perseverance.

Looking Ahead

In the next chapter, we'll explore what happens when you combine those two forces, the depth of experience and the breadth of structured learning, and apply them to real-world challenges. Because knowledge in isolation is only potential. Knowledge tested and applied becomes wisdom's raw material.

Chapter Takeaway:

Experience may give you a map, but structured learning adds new continents. Formal education, short courses, or even mentorship don't compete with experience: they expand it. The real measure isn't the credential itself, but how learning stretches your mind, equips you with new tools, and keeps you growing long after the course is done.

CHAPTER 5

WISDOM BEYOND THE COMFORT ZONE

"Not all classrooms have four walls."

— *Unknown**

Wisdom rarely arrives with a syllabus. More often, it appears when we step into territory we don't yet know how to navigate: the moments where curiosity, necessity, or stubborn persistence push us beyond the familiar. These are the lessons that stay with us because we had to reach for them, wrestle with them, or discover them through trial and error.

This isn't a new idea. History is full of people who stretched beyond their comfort zones to learn something no book could teach. Benjamin Franklin, a runaway apprentice, built his education in printing, science, and diplomacy by seeking

---

*If this quote resonates with you, I encourage you to research experiential learning. There are several papers and books that help bring this concept alive.

out mentors and experimenting constantly. Mary Anning, a working-class girl with no formal training, became one of the most important fossil hunters in history.

Across centuries and circumstances, the pattern is the same: those who step beyond the familiar often change the world. Hedy Lamarr, who was celebrated as a glamorous actress, co-developed a secure communications system that later influenced Wi-Fi, Bluetooth, and GPS. George Washington Carver, born into slavery, transformed agriculture through a lifetime of experimentation and innovation with crops such as peanuts, sweet potatoes, and soybeans.

Their worlds expanded because they dared to cross the line between the known and the unknown. While each of their stories stands on its own, they also show how informal discovery often lays the foundation for more structured breakthroughs later on. Their stories are extraordinary, but the same principles echo in smaller ways in everyday life, including mine.

Challenging the Limits Others Set for You

In grade school, an art teacher told me I had no talent: a comment I believed for years. That single remark nearly shut the door on creativity, just as early critics once dismissed Mary Anning's fossil discoveries because she was poor and uneducated. Yet Anning kept collecting, studying, and sharing her work until the scientific world had no choice but to listen. In my own way, I eventually found my creative voice on stage, in voice acting, and in the craft of woodturning: proving that art, like learning, is never defined by one person's opinion.

Wisdom reminds us that one voice can wound, but it takes reflection and persistence to decide whose voice will define our path.

Challenging the Limits You Set for Yourself

But not every barrier comes from someone else's judgment. Sometimes, the limits are the ones we imagine for ourselves. My uncle Garry, just two years older than me, and I stayed in touch whenever we could. In the 1970s, long-distance phone calls were expensive, and our experiments with CB radio couldn't bridge the distance. So we set ourselves a challenge: earn our ham radio licenses.

We bought workbooks and cassette tapes for Morse Code training from Radio Shack, and within a year, we were talking to each other "over the air." Two years later, we both achieved our Advanced licenses, opening a whole new world of connections. The limits were real: costly phone calls, inadequate equipment, obstacles that could have stopped us. But curiosity, paired with a shared goal, pushed us past them into skills and communities we never imagined.

Pause and Reflect

- Think back over the last few years.

- What is one skill or insight you've gained without formal training, something learned through curiosity, observation, trial and error, or simply saying yes to an unexpected opportunity?

- How has that lesson shaped the way you work, create, or live?

- What might you be able to teach others from it?

Giving Back Before You Feel Ready

That same push beyond the comfortable showed up in my karate training. Black Belts were expected to teach without pay: a principle rooted in the belief that mastery carries the responsibility to give back. At first, the idea felt intimidating. But stepping into that teaching role taught me that influence isn't about titles; it's about service, humility, and leaving something better than you found it. What I learned informally in that dojo would later inform my work in structured educational settings.

Learning by Watching

Some lessons arrive simply by observing someone who does it better. I'd struggled for months to back up our 5th wheel trailer until one evening, at a truck stop, I watched truckers ease their rigs into tight spaces. They began straightening earlier than I did, correcting by aligning the trailer first. The next morning, my problem was gone.

Benjamin Franklin used this same principle on a grander scale. He watched storms, studied lightning, and then dared to test what he observed with his famous kite-and-key experiment. Careful observation didn't just teach him something new; it unlocked insights that still shape our understanding of electricity.

Careful watching, when paired with action, can shrink the learning curve dramatically. And when supported by structured study, as Franklin and others showed, observation becomes innovation.

Trial, Error, and the Push to Improve

I entered teaching at SAIT with industry experience, but I had almost no idea how to run a classroom. Those first mistakes felt like they might cost me my career. Instead, my leaders encouraged me to treat them as stepping stones, much like George Washington Carver, who tested thousands of crop varieties before finding the ones that would restore soil health. Each failure pushed him closer to success.

My own early stumbles in the classroom led me to workshops, conferences, and eventually formal study. What began as fumbling in the dark became a deliberate integration of informal lessons and structured learning: a pairing that continues to shape my work today.

Saying Yes Before You're Certain

Taking on the role of camp host was one of those "say yes now, figure it out later" moments. We thought we knew what to expect, but the reality stretched us in ways we hadn't anticipated. Some days, I felt like giving up, echoing what Hedy Lamarr must have felt when stepping into the male-dominated world of wartime engineering. But staying the course revealed new strengths and perspectives I wouldn't trade.

In hindsight, saying yes before I felt ready was also a rehearsal for how I approach formal opportunities: knowing that growth often comes from commitment first, confidence later.

Informal learning rarely announces itself. It hides in the moments when we give back, when curiosity pulls us forward, when observation reveals a better way, when failure becomes a teacher, and when we step through an unfamiliar door without knowing exactly what's on the other side.

The pattern is always the same: leaving the safe ground expands the territory of your understanding. And when you later map that expanded territory onto structured learning, the result is a kind of wisdom that neither path could produce alone.

In the next chapter, we'll explore how to merge the open-ended discovery of informal learning with the focus and discipline of formal education – because while either can change you, only together can they transform you. And sometimes, their collision sparks the most challenging but most valuable lessons of all.

Chapter Takeaway:

Stepping beyond the comfort zone is where informal learning thrives. Whether it's giving back before you feel ready, pushing past limits set by others or yourself, learning by watching, or failing forward, each step into the unfamiliar expands your capacity. Informal discovery doesn't replace structured learning, but it prepares the ground for it. Wisdom grows when courage meets curiosity; when you risk leaving the familiar and find yourself transformed.

CHAPTER 6

WHEN KNOWLEDGE
AND EXPERIENCE COLLIDE

"It ain't what you don't know that gets you into trouble. It's what you know for sure that just ain't so."

— *Mark Twain**

Experience is a stubborn teacher. It'll keep handing you the same lesson until you believe it's the whole truth. Which is great! Until the day it isn't. Then you're stuck deciding: trust the way you've always done it, or try something new and untested? Sometimes that choice feels like swapping out a well-worn pair of hiking boots for a pair you have never walked in. Which happened to me earlier this summer. During the first three weeks of excruciating pain while breaking in my newest pair of boots, I often wondered 'if it was worth it'!

---

*https://www.thinkindependent.com.au/aint-dont-know-gets-trouble/

(Spoiler: it was, but my feet still haven't forgiven me.) But the trail was changing under my feet, and I recognized the adage, "short-term pain for long-term gain." The same years of "knowing how things are done" that keep you confident can also keep you blind. What happens when the method that's always worked collides with the evidence that says it's wrong? Do you trust what's familiar, or do you step into the uncertainty of something new?

The Lighting Grid Lesson

For several years, I taught theatre courses in a small Blackbox theatre: the kind of space so close that the first row of audience members could rest their feet on the stage during performances. Which, by the way, is something we discouraged. The lighting grid hung low by professional standards, reachable with a rolling staircase like the ones you'd see in a hardware store. Only much shorter. We didn't have Broadway resources. We owned a total of 20 lighting instruments. As a result, because we had so many different groups performing, we lit the stage in zones and had the students block their scenes to match the newly formed pools of light. Nobody tripped, nobody fell. It wasn't glamorous, but it worked. My track record was clean, and I believed it was safe.

Then the campus introduced new safety protocols: anyone working at height had to wear a harness, have a spotter, and secure the stairs with a safety chain when not in use. Sensible rules? Sure: on paper. To me, however, it felt like overkill. I had been hanging lights for more than 20 years without an incident. In my head, this was just another example of needless bureaucracy. Why ask a student to stay late so that I could clip in a few lights?

One evening, I ignored the policy. Alone, I rolled the staircase into position, climbed up, and reached for the grid. Standing on my tiptoes, I tightened a clamp and felt something cinch around my neck. It took a half second for my brain to register: my tie. Caught.

Pause and Reflect

- When have you trusted "the way it's always been done" instead of testing something new?

- What finally convinced you to change – or what kept you from it?

- Where might "safe enough" be blinding you today?

Not choking, but tight enough to make me stop breathing. The possibility that I couldn't free myself came into focus, stark and immediate. I reached up. Unhooked the tie. Climbed down. My pulse was pounding an AC/DC drumbeat in my ears, the faint smell of stage dust lingering in the rafters.

That was the last time I dismissed a safety rule just because I thought I'd "never needed it." My years without an accident had felt like proof that my way was the right way. In truth, it turned out, my "safe enough" was just a spotlight shining on my own narrow experience. The rest of the stage was still clouded in shadows. It was also the last time I wore a tie in the theatre.

The lesson wasn't about ladders or lighting. It was about how experience can cast obscurities over judgment, convincing us that what we've seen is all there is to see.

That wasn't the last time my tried-and-true methods got called into question. The classroom, as it turned out, could be just as risky as a rolling staircase.

Teaching and Learning Styles

When I first began teaching at SAIT, I defaulted to the style I had grown up with: the instructor at the front, students in rows, and a clear lecture from start to finish. It was orderly, efficient, and, at least in my mind, effective.

Then came professional development workshops on "active learning": peer teaching, collaborative problem-solving, and hands-on activities. The research was clear: students retained more when they were engaged.

So, I tried it. Chaos followed. Off-topic chatter. A few students disengaged. Control slipped through my fingers, and my old instincts shouted: *Go back to order. Go back to control.* Honestly, I wanted to. But the research lingered like an unanswered question: was my trusted method really the best way to help them learn?

That tension, between lived experience and new evidence, wasn't just mine. History is full of moments when entrenched practice collided with disruptive knowledge. Most of them had much bigger consequences than an undisciplined classroom.

Semmelweis and the Handwashing Revolution*

In the 1840s, Dr. Ignaz Semmelweis worked in a maternity clinic in Vienna, a place where too many mothers were dying of childbed fever. The prevailing wisdom of the time, rooted in centuries of medical practice, blamed "miasma," or bad air, for the disease. Physicians moved freely from one patient to another without changing clothes, let alone washing their hands.

Semmelweis noticed something disturbing: women cared for by doctors and medical students were far more likely to die than those attended by midwives. The difference, he realized, was that doctors often came directly from performing autopsies to delivering babies.

---

*https://www.scientificamerican.com/blog/guest-blog/as-scientists-get-political-public-health-offers-a-blueprint-for-success/?WT.mc_id=SA_TW_POLE_BLOG

He tested a radical idea: require all medical staff to wash their hands with a chlorine solution before examining patients. Death rates plummeted almost immediately.

The evidence was undeniable, but many of Semmelweis's colleagues weren't buying it. Decades of "safe" practice, pride in their skill, and the weight of tradition outweighed a bucket of chlorine water. To admit he was right meant acknowledging that their actions had contributed to countless unnecessary deaths.

Semmelweis's findings eventually became the cornerstone of modern infection control, but not before years of resistance and ridicule cost lives. His story reminds us that progress depends not just on discovering evidence, but on letting go of the practices we trust.

Closing Reflection

Whether it's boots, a tie, or a bucket of chlorine water, sometimes the thing that saves you is the thing you least want to try. There's constant negotiation between what experience tells you and what formal knowledge demands. Sometimes the familiar feels safest; other times, it blinds you to better ways.

The tension in these stories is intentional. It's the space where growth begins, where neither experience nor knowledge gets the final word without being tested. In the next chapter, I'll step into that uneasy middle ground, exploring how to question both sides and decide, with clearer eyes, which to trust.

> ## *Chapter Takeaway:*
> *When experience and knowledge collide, growth depends not on choosing one, but on letting each correct the other.*

CHAPTER 7

THE SPACE BETWEEN CONTROL AND CHAOS

*"You can't control the wind,
but you can adjust your sails.**

In the last chapter, I left things unresolved: experience on one side, learned knowledge on the other, each tugging for dominance. Let the contest begin. Which side will end up face-first in the mud?

This time, we step into the space between those forces: the middle ground where freedom meets structure, and where leaders, teachers, and even dog owners must decide how much room to give for exploration and how much to hold back for safety. This is simple to state but harder to practice: enough

---

*This quote has been attributed to several authors. In my research, the earliest example I can find is Cora L. V. Hatch (1859)

structure to keep things from falling apart, enough freedom to let people, or dogs, find their way.

Control, Freedom, and the Space Between

A short leash feels safe. You can predict, direct, and contain what happens. But it also limits discovery. A long leash invites exploration, but it carries risk: the dog might tangle himself; the kite might crash. The art lies in knowing how much slack to give and, like any good fisherman, when to reel it in.

I did not always see it that way. My farm-life instincts equated control with safety. Short leads, tight reins, firm boundaries: those were my trusted tools. Honestly, if you've ever tried to lead a 2,300-pound Charolais bull over any distance, you will understand why I prefer the short lead attached to a nose ring.

Over time, I learned that control may keep order, but it can also stifle growth.

Testing and Adjusting in the Classroom

That pressure between experience and new learning followed me from the previous chapter straight into my teaching. But instead of retreating to my old habits, I tried again: this time with intention.

I kept a short lecture to cover the essentials, then shifted to a group exercise: write a 60-second promotional spot for a fictional radio station event, match the brand voice, and perform it live.

It was far from perfect. A few off-topic tangents. A few hesitant silences. But something had shifted. I could now see who understood the material without guessing.

Over the weeks, I alternated between lecture and activity. Lectures provided the "what" and "why"; activities offered the "how" and "what it feels like." Over time, even my lecture style shifted. Instead of "lectures," they became stories and examples from industry. Before long, I saw a very positive response. The students started referring to those moments as "story time with Steve"! (Their label, not mine.) It was at that stage of my teaching career that purpose replaced routine.

Eventually, I stopped seeing myself as an industry guy "teaching industry" and began to see myself as an educator, facilitating learning. In my view, teachers fill vessels; educators help students shape their own path. The realization that students require ownership and autonomy became central to my work in the classroom and later in my doctoral research.

Letting Out the Leash

The same lesson appeared outside the classroom. On the farm, dogs roamed free, and livestock were led with short, sturdy lines. Safety meant control.

When I moved to the city, bylaws required leashes of a set length; in our town, that was 6 feet (1.8 meters). In a quiet park, I tested one twice the usual length with Morrie and noticed something surprising.

Almost immediately, his pace slowed, his nose dropped to the ground, and he followed scent trails with calm focus. The pulling stopped. My shoulders relaxed. The walk shifted from a test of strength to a shared exploration. I wasn't losing control; I was redefining it. What I came to recognize was that the opportunity to sniff was a reward for Morrie. One found in his environment. And here's a bonus: 45 minutes of sniffing in the early evening means a tired dog who puts himself to bed. Win!

Since then, I've adapted: short leash in busy and required spaces and long lead in open areas. The science was right, but so was my lived experience. The wisdom lies in knowing when to apply which and being willing to test assumptions.

Be the Kite

I once facilitated a drama class where students worked in groups of ten to create two pieces: a structured improv and an interpretive movement piece. Stepping out of the theatre for a few minutes, I returned to find two students on stage, arms raised, swaying in silence like windblown scarecrows.

I watched for a few minutes, but for the life of me, I could not figure out what they were doing.

"What's this?" I asked.

"We're trying to synchronize kite-flying," they said.

It looked awkward. I told them, "Be the kite." And then explained that real kites never move in perfect unison; each responds differently, even to the same wind.

They took the advice, and the piece came alive. Later, one of the group members said, "I see what you did there. You're the one holding the string, and we are the kites. And you are letting us ride the wind." I'm not sure what prompted the comment, but it has stayed with me as a perfect metaphor for leadership: giving enough freedom to explore while still offering a line of safety.

The principle was the same with Morrie's leash. Farm instinct told me to hold him close; research told me to give him space. The art was in knowing when to guide and when to let go.

What to Carry Forward

Reflection isn't about reliving the past; instead, it's about choosing what to carry forward and what to leave behind. Without it, even our best intentions can trap us in old patterns.

I once knew a woman who had worked for a largely self-taught entrepreneur who'd found some success in the publishing

---

Pause and Reflect

We repeat until we reflect.

What patterns have you repeated — in leading, teaching, parenting, or another walk of life — that you later realized came from someone else's influence rather than your own choice?

---

industry. His methods were flawed—and at times, troubling. She recognized his failings, yet when she struck out on her own, echoes of those same destructive patterns crept into her leadership. It was as if experience alone had imprinted itself so deeply that, even when she knew better, she repeated the very behaviours she had once criticized.

We parent as we were parented, we lead as we were led, we teach as we were taught; unless we pause to reflect and choose to break the chain.

Earlier in this book, I called this the experience loop: the repetition of unexamined methods, mistaking familiarity for wisdom. Here, we see how easily that loop becomes a trap.

Experience without reflection often locks us in cycles. We carry forward not only the lessons that worked but also the dysfunctions we've witnessed. Reflection is what allows us to break the cycle: to ask not just "What did I see?" but "What should I carry forward, and what should I leave behind?"

This is the danger of experience without reflection: we may produce the very behaviours we know are broken. Reflection is the pause that allows us to break the cycle and build something wiser.

Reflection shows us what not to carry forward: often more powerful than knowing what to pursue.

Humble Reflection

Reflection is powerful, but without humility, it can slip into self-congratulation. I've seen leaders reflect on their decisions only to turn the exercise into a highlight reel of their successes. That isn't wisdom: it's branding.

Humble reflection asks a different set of questions: *Where did I fall short? What did I miss? What did others see that I didn't?* It resists polishing the story and admits the cracks instead. That kind of honesty is uncomfortable, but it's also what makes reflection transformative.

> **Pause and Reflect**
>
> We often polish our stories to highlight what went well. Humble reflection asks harder questions:
>
> - Where did I fall short?
> - What did I miss that others noticed?
> - How did my choices affect people differently than I expected?
>
> True wisdom grows when reflection is paired with humility.

The Common Thread

Whether in a classroom, on a sidewalk, or in a theatre, growth happens when there's room to move yet enough structure to prevent chaos. Too much control stifles. Too little invites trouble. The line, whether a leash, a lesson plan, a leadership boundary, or an invisible string, exists not to restrict, but to connect us with the very thing we're trying to lead.

Next, we'll see what happens when letting go doesn't just create growth: it sparks transformation.

> ## *Chapter Takeaway:*
>
> *Growth lives in the space between control and chaos. Too much control smothers, too little destabilizes. Wisdom is knowing when to hold tight, when to let go, and when to adjust the line.*

CHAPTER 8

THE COMPLETION OF WISDOM

"A bird sitting on a tree is never afraid of the branch breaking, because its trust is not on the branch but on its own wings."

— *Charlie Wardle**

In the last chapter, we explored the balance between control and freedom: the "longer leash" or "kite string" that lets people explore while still staying connected. Now we take the next step: seeing what happens when experience and knowledge are not in competition, but in partnership. This is where the strands of doing and knowing twist together into something more substantial: wisdom.

---

*https://www.goodreads.com/author/quotes/7946971. Charlie_Wardle

When Letting Go Changes the Leader Too

The first time I loosened my grip, on a leash, a kite string, or a lesson plan, I expected only small shifts: a little more freedom, a touch of independence. But sometimes letting go changes everything.

I'd already learned this with Morrie on a longer leash: sometimes letting go changes you, too. My pace slowed. My awareness widened. I saw the trail through his curiosity, rather than my destination-driven agenda. At first, I'd quip to passersby, as Morrie buried his nose in something, "Just stopping to smell the roses." That became, "Just stopping to smell everything." Eventually, I arrived at, "I love that he finds everything so interesting."

The same thing happened in the classroom. When I told my students to "be the kite," I thought I was adjusting the dynamic. I didn't foresee the deeper conversations, the creative risks, and the ownership they would take over their work. When students felt the work was theirs, not just mine, they cared more about both the journey and the outcome. My role was to create a space where they had the freedom to steer but enough guidance to keep moving forward. That mix sparked genuine engagement. I was equally fascinated by my own reaction to their learning; it allowed me to stop and, like Morrie, find everything so interesting.

The truth is simple but profound: intentional letting go doesn't just benefit the one being led: it transforms the leader too.

Experience Perfects

To this point, we've wrestled with the limitations of experience alone and celebrated the opening power of knowledge. But wisdom is not born from either in isolation. There's a Latin phrase that captures this perfectly:

Experientia perfectum — "Experience perfects."

This doesn't mean experience is flawless. It means experience completes. It adds shading, texture, and context that knowledge alone cannot provide.

Consider reading a map: you can memorize the symbols and understand scale: that's knowledge. But until you've been caught on a trail at dusk with the wind rising, you don't honestly know how to navigate under pressure. That's where experience perfects knowledge.

Or reverse it: you might have driven the same road a hundred times: that's experience. But without understanding how wet pavement changes braking distance, your reaction in a sudden storm may be dangerously slow. That's where knowledge perfects experience.

On the trail with Morrie, I trust the map; he trusts the scents and terrain. When we combine both, we find our way. When we rely only on one, we sometimes end up in blackberry thickets; or worse, admitting we're lost and calling Libby for a rescue (he mutters under his breath).

The point is this: knowledge sketches the lines; experience fills them in. Together, they create the complete picture.

Experientia Perfectum

"Experience perfects"

*It does not mean experience is perfect.
It means experience completes.*

Experientia perfectum is a Latin phrase that captures the partnership between knowledge and experience.
It's not about proving one is better — it's about recognizing that each is incomplete without the other.

Theory without application	Repetition without learning
Can be precise but untested	Can be reliable but outdated
Draws the map	Walks the trail

Ask yourself: What happens when you rely on one without the other?

The more willing you are to ask that question, the closer you move toward wisdom.

Two Illustrative Examples

1. THE MAP AND THE TRAIL

Knowledge First: You can read a topographic map, understand contour lines, and estimate travel time.

Experience Completes It: You've been caught on the ridge at dusk with a storm rolling in. You know the feel of the wind before rain, the way footing changes on wet rock, and how quickly the temperature drops. The Lesson: Experience perfects knowledge by adding instincts and nuance that can't be found in a book.

2. THE ROAD AND THE STORM

Experience First: You've driven the same road to work for twenty years.

Knowledge Completes It: Understanding how wet pavement changes braking distance means you react differently, faster, in a sudden downpour.

A Lesson from 1970

In 1970, I took a class in astronomy. My first project was to build a working telescope. I was in grade eight, and just like that, I was hooked on space and, soon thereafter, science fiction novels.

That same year, the world was riveted by Apollo 13, the mission that was supposed to land on the Moon but instead became a masterclass in survival. An oxygen tank exploded on the way there, crippling the spacecraft and forcing the crew to abandon the Moon landing. "Houston, we've had a problem" became one of the most famous understatements in history.*

Note, this is what was said. The line was changed for the movie!

The astronauts had experience: they knew their spacecraft, they had trained for emergencies, and they could stay calm under pressure. The engineers at NASA had knowledge: they understood the systems down to the smallest bolt, could calculate oxygen burn rates, and knew how to reroute power.

Neither group could have succeeded alone. The engineers devised the fix; the astronauts built it under pressure. Apollo 13 never landed on the Moon, but it made it safely home because *experientia perfectum* played out in real time.

The lesson: wisdom emerges when knowledge and experience are trusted to work together.

From Compliance to Ownership

When leaders, teachers, or mentors step back, something remarkable happens: people step forward.

With Morrie, that meant he could choose his own route around a tree or pause to sniff without tension in the line. In the classroom, it meant students made creative decisions without waiting for my approval.

But there's a flip side. Early in my teaching, I once gave a group too much freedom too soon. They had enthusiasm but lacked the skills to navigate the task, and frustration set in quickly. The result was disengagement, not ownership. I learned that freedom works best when it's matched with readiness. I also recognized that part of my role was to prepare people for the responsibility I was about to hand them.

The difference between compliance and ownership goes beyond skill. Compliance meets expectations; ownership exceeds them. The best outcomes often come when people have both the trust to try and the support to recover if they stumble.

The Gift of the Unexpected

Control gives you predictable results, but rarely transformative ones. Letting go makes space for what you could not have planned.

That was true whether it was students learning to "be the kite," Morrie discovering the calm of a longer leash, or the Apollo 13 crew turning a disaster into a triumph. The surprise wasn't only in what they accomplished, it was also in what I discovered: new ways to notice, to adapt, and to trust.

Pause and Reflect

Think about a time in your life when you relied only on experience and later realized you needed more knowledge — or when you relied only on knowledge and later realized you needed more experience.

- How would combining both have changed the outcome?

- Where in your life right now could you "loosen the leash" just enough to allow growth — for someone else and for yourself?

The payoff of trust is not just better results for others: it's deeper growth for yourself.

But even in this completion, another challenge remains: what do you do when letting go leads somewhere unexpected – or somewhere you didn't want to go? In the next chapter, I'll explore the art of responding when freedom produces not just surprise, but actual change: for better or for worse.

Chapter Takeaway:

Knowledge without experience is theory. Experience without knowledge is repetition without growth. Together, they complete each other. This is experientia perfectum: *the synthesis that transforms doing and knowing into wisdom.*

CHAPTER 9

APPLYING WISDOM IN THE REAL WORLD

"Knowledge is knowing what to say. Wisdom is knowing whether or not to say it."

— *Socrates**

In the last chapter, we explored experientia perfectum: the completeness that comes when knowledge and experience work together. That partnership is the foundation of wisdom. But wisdom, like a Tim Hortons Double Chocolate Donut, doesn't do much if you just admire it from across the room. You have to take a bite.

This chapter is about taking that synthesis and putting it to work in everyday life: in decisions, relationships, and leadership.

---

*It is very difficult to find the exact source of this phrase. However, the sentiment is consistent with the self-awareness teachings of Socrates.

From Concept to Practice

One of the easiest traps after learning a big idea is assuming you've mastered it just because you understand it. But wisdom doesn't stick unless you act on it.

Applying *experientia perfectum* is not about suddenly becoming a flawless decision-maker. It's about developing habits that pull from both wells: the lived experiences that shape your instincts, and the knowledge that sharpens them.

In the last chapter, I used the image of a wet road to show how knowledge sharpens experience. Now picture that same road in winter. Your experience tells you where the sharp turns are, while your knowledge reminds you to slow down before you reach them. That's how wisdom works: the same road, new season, both perspectives working together.

Arena 1: Decision-Making Under Pressure

In high-pressure moments, most of us default to one of two modes: we either act purely on instinct or we freeze while collecting more and more data. Wisdom lives in the balance.

Example 1 — The $94,000 Paper Weight

The call came mid-morning: *"You have an extra $94,000 for Film and Video Production: but you need the proposal in within two hours."*

As Academic Chair at SAIT, I was familiar with our standard process. Budget allotments arrived weeks in advance; we'd meet with faculty, prioritize requests, and make sure every program got something. In Film and Video Production (FVP), that usually meant buying a dozen smaller items. It was safe, predictable, and never got us closer to their dream: an Arri Alexa cinema camera, the gold standard in the industry and far beyond our regular budget.

I gathered the faculty and presented two options: either allocate the funds across the smaller items or combine them with our existing budget to purchase part of the Alexa. Just the body. No lenses, no power supply, nothing to make it functional. They looked at me like I'd lost it. *"What will we do with a camera we can't use?"*

Here's where *experientia perfectum* kicked in. Past purchases taught me that incomplete equipment often received priority the following year. I gambled on that pattern, hoping colleagues would see the logic. To my relief, they agreed, and the risk paid off.

For a year, the Alexa body sat proudly on my desk: the most expensive paperweight on campus. And the next year? FVP was the proud owner of their dream camera.

Example 2 — Miracle on the Hudson

Not all high-pressure decisions give you hours. Some give you seconds.

On January 15, 2009, Captain Chesley "Sully" Sullenberger was flying US Airways Flight 1549 out of New York's LaGuardia Airport. Just three minutes after takeoff, a flock of geese struck both engines, and suddenly the plane was powerless: an Airbus A320 turned glider, carrying 155 lives.

Air traffic control urged Sully to turn back toward LaGuardia. On paper, that was the "standard" play. But Sully knew the math. The altitude, speed, and trajectory made a return impossible. A turn would almost certainly end in disaster in a densely populated city.

In a matter of seconds, he drew on decades of flying experience, simulator training, and his calm judgment. He made the call: ditch in the Hudson River. It wasn't in any manual. It wasn't in the plan. But it was the only way to save lives.

Three and a half minutes after the bird strike, Flight 1549 landed safely on the river. Everyone survived. It became known as the "Miracle on the Hudson."

Sully's decision illustrates what wisdom under pressure looks like. Pure instinct risks panic. Pure analysis costs time. Wisdom lives in the balance: just enough data, just enough intuition, and the courage to act.

Whether it's a $100,000 camera or a $100-million powerless jet, the principle is the same: wisdom is less about time on the clock and more about using both head and gut in the time you've got.

How to Apply Decision-Making Under Pressure

1. **Match your pace to the moment.** Some decisions give you days, some hours, and some only seconds. Read the moment and adjust.

2. **Check both instinct and evidence.** Even in a quick pause, ask:

    o   What do I know from experience?

    o   What does the data tell me right now?

3. **Decide and commit.** In high-pressure moments, half-decisions are often worse than wrong ones. Once you choose, move with conviction.

Pocket Takeaway

Under pressure, wisdom means reading the moment, checking both head and gut, and then committing fully.

Arena 2: Navigating Conflict

If wisdom steadies us in the cockpit or the boardroom, it's tested just as much in the hallway: in moments of conflict.

Of all the arenas in this book, conflict is the one I've wrestled with the most. I know I've made a difference for many people through empathy, patience, and understanding. But when the conflict was my own, the emotions often came too fast, too strong, and too loud.

Looking back, I can see that many of my hardest leadership lessons were learned in the middle of conflict. In my previous book, *Lessons in Leadership*, I shared how I sometimes mishandled it: letting frustration take over, saying things I wished I could take back. The wisdom came later, after the sting had faded and the reflection had begun.

Strangely enough, I was often better at helping others manage conflict than handling it myself. When two staff members were at odds, I learned not to referee their arguments or force a compromise too quickly. Instead, I'd ask a single question:

"What is in the best interest of our students?"

That one line reframed the conversation. Instead of battling for their position, people could see the bigger purpose. Often, the conflict dissolved in seconds. They didn't need me to declare a winner. They just needed a reminder of why they were here.

The paradox of conflict is that it rarely feels good in the moment, but it almost always carries a lesson. For me, the lesson was clear: wisdom in conflict doesn't come from avoiding it, nor from dominating it. It comes from slowing the rush of emotions long enough to return to purpose.

How to Apply Navigating Conflict

1. **Name your trigger.** If conflict makes your emotions flare, notice it before it takes over. Naming it creates a pause.

2. **Reframe the focus.** Ask: What's in the best interest of the larger purpose? Whether it's students, customers, or the mission, shared goals cut through personal differences.

3. **Choose calm over right.** The calmest person in the room often carries the most influence. Aim to lower the heat, not win the argument.

Pocket Takeaway

In conflict, wisdom means slowing the rush of emotion, refocusing on shared purpose, and choosing calm over being right.

Arena 3: Leading and Mentoring Others

Of course, wisdom isn't just about resolving conflict. It's also about building others up before conflict even starts: through leadership and mentoring.

Wisdom in leadership often shows up as knowing when to speak, when to listen, and when to step back entirely.

A few years after I took up the hobby of woodturning, I experienced one of my most memorable mentoring moments. I had taken some short courses and joined the local woodturning guild, where members were always ready to share tips, offer one-on-one guidance, or encourage each other. Many in the guild also looked for opportunities to give back, such as the

Beads of Courage project, which provides hand-turned boxes for children coping with serious illness to store their beads of bravery.

I was eager to contribute. After many bowls, pepper grinders, and "magic wands," I felt ready. I bought a beautiful piece of wood, mounted it on my lathe, and turned what I thought was my best piece yet: a box with a perfectly fitted lid, polished smooth, with an emblem embedded in the handle. I must have opened and closed it a dozen times that night, proud of my creation.

By morning, the pride was gone. The lid no longer fit. The box itself had warped out of round: unusable overnight.

At the next guild meeting, I approached Kai, one of the guild's best woodturners and an intimidating but generous mentor. I showed him my disaster in a shopping bag, and he walked me through a quiet discovery process.

- Where did you get the blank?
- So this was made from a bowl blank, not a box blank?
- And what's the grain orientation of a bowl?
- And what do we all know about side grain?

The answer came to me: *wood moves; side-grain* bowls warp. End-grain boxes hold their shape. I had learned the lesson myself, with Kai nudging me to the realization.

He didn't stop there. Kai debriefed, complimenting the turn, wall thickness, finish, and design, then challenged me: *"Now make another, with the right blank."*

That was mentorship at its best: guiding discovery, affirming strengths, and issuing the next challenge.

How to Apply Leading and Mentoring Others

1. **Gauge readiness.** Give freedom in proportion to skill and confidence.

2. **Coach, don't control.** Guide discovery rather than dictate answers.

3. **Debrief and affirm.** Review together, highlight strengths, and set the next challenge.

Pocket Takeaway

Great mentors don't just give answers: they guide discovery, affirm strengths, and set the next challenge.

Small Moments Count Too

Not every test of wisdom looks dramatic. Most of the time, it shows up in the quiet, everyday choices. It might be choosing not to correct someone on a trivial mistake because you know it would embarrass them, or taking a new route on a walk with Morrie because of the combined knowledge of the weather and the experience of how he reacts in new environments.

It's in these smaller, almost invisible decisions that wisdom quietly builds trust, strengthens relationships, and makes life a little smoother.

A MINI TOOLKIT FOR APPLYING WISDOM

- **Pause before acting.** Give both instinct and analysis a voice.
- **Seek the second perspective.** Ask: *Who knows something I don't?*
- **Test before committing.** Try small-scale experiments before big decisions.
- **Reflect afterward.** Ask: *What did I know? What did I learn? How will it shape my next choice?*

Closing Reflection

Applying *experientia perfectum* isn't about grand gestures. It's about weaving the partnership of knowledge and experience into daily choices: so often and so naturally that it becomes who you are.

Wisdom isn't something you keep on a shelf. It's the tool you carry into the workshop of the real world: shaping every decision, big or small.

And in the next chapter, we'll look at how wisdom doesn't just guide the choices of today but also shapes the kind of person you are becoming tomorrow.

Chapter Takeaway:

Wisdom under pressure isn't about instinct alone or analysis alone. It's the habit of drawing on both — your lived experience and your learned knowledge — and applying them to choices big and small. The more you practice it, the more naturally wisdom becomes part of your everyday decisions.

CHAPTER 10

FROM WISDOM TO LEGACY

Sapientia est vitae usus.
"Wisdom is the practice of life."

We have walked through nine arenas of experience: decisions under pressure, conflict, leadership, teaching, slowing down, and even those small, invisible moments with a dog on a trail. At every turn, the pattern was the same: experience plus knowledge, shaped by reflection, led to wisdom. But wisdom is not an endpoint. It's not the trophy at the end of the race. It's what you carry forward, what you pass along, and what others pick up from you – sometimes without you even knowing.

Knowledge is Power.
— Francis Bacon

Experience shapes how we see.

Reflection shapes what we learn from what we see.

Wisdom is the compass that shows us where — and whether — to use it.

Pause and Reflect

- When in your own life has knowledge given you the power to act — but you weren't sure which way to turn?

- How have experience and reflection helped you point that power in the right direction?

- What might change if you thought of wisdom not as a distant peak, but as a compass guiding your daily steps?

Wisdom as a Daily Practice

One of the quiet discoveries in writing this book was that wisdom is not dramatic most of the time. It's usually subtle: the pause before you reply in frustration, the choice to walk away rather than escalate, the act of really listening when someone else needs space. Wisdom is learned in the grand arenas, but lived in the daily ones.

From Personal to Communal

If knowledge is individual and experience is personal, wisdom is communal. It connects. It becomes most valuable when it serves others: a student who sees their potential because you stepped back at the right moment, a colleague who calms down because you asked the right question, a child or grandchild who remembers not just what you said, but how you lived.

The Thread of Purpose

Wisdom is always tethered to a purpose beyond ourselves. When we connect decisions back to that larger purpose, the path becomes clearer. It works in classrooms, boardrooms, and even at the kitchen table.

Small Legacies

Legacy is not always about writing books or leading organizations. Sometimes it's about those small, Morrie-like moments: choosing to flop down in the grass and watch the sky instead of racing to the next thing. Those quiet choices may leave a greater legacy than any lecture or formal training.

As Maya Angelou reminds us, *"I've learned that people will forget what you said, people will forget what you did, but people will never forget how you made them feel."**

**Often attributed to Maya Angelou; earliest verified phrasing appears in circulation before her publications and is also linked to variations by others (e.g., Carl W. Buehner). Quotation included here as widely attributed.*

A Different Perspective

Wisdom doesn't only reveal itself by presence; it also shows itself by absence. The opposite of wisdom is not ignorance, but authority without grounding. I once reported to a leader whose authority came not from knowledge or leadership ability, but from position alone. The results were predictable: decisions made without grounding, and a culture where authority was mistaken for competence.

When leadership rests on position alone, it is fragile. It may appear stable in the moment, but without the support of knowledge and reflection, it eventually harms both people and organizations. We've seen positional leadership play out everywhere: from small teams to large institutions, even on the world stage. What I've come to see is that wisdom in leadership isn't about securing control; it's about creating conditions where others can succeed.

When leadership is rooted in position rather than competence, the structure may look solid, but it is built on sand. Wisdom, by contrast, rests on a foundation of experience, knowledge, and reflection: a structure strong enough to endure.

The Intangibles

If wisdom rested only on the three pillars, life might unfold predictably. But anyone who has been on this planet for a while knows better: life surprises us. Sometimes what carries us through is not a polished pillar, but an intangible force that refuses to be diagrammed on a page.

Luck

Also known as the opportunity you didn't earn, the break you didn't plan, the timing you couldn't control. Entire careers have been shaped by being in the right place at the right time. A near miss has redirected whole lives.

My own radio career began with persistence and hard work, but my first full-time gig came because I happened to be in the room when someone else got fired. The boss pointed at me and said, "Get in the control room and finish his shift." That was luck, pure and simple.

Wisdom doesn't eliminate luck; it acknowledges it. The wise accept good fortune with humility and bad fortune without bitterness. Ignoring luck makes us arrogant; recognizing it makes us grateful.

Instinct

Call it a gut feeling, intuition, or the quiet voice inside. Instinct often arises when experience and reflection haven't yet caught up. You don't always know why you feel pulled in a particular direction, but usually that instinct proves correct. It isn't magic; it's the sum of patterns your mind has absorbed beneath the surface.

Wisdom lies in knowing when to trust that voice and when to test it.

Common Sense

And finally, common sense: that plainspoken cousin of reflection. It doesn't require a degree, and it doesn't always bow to theory. It asks grounding questions: "Does this really make sense? Would I want to be treated this way? What's the obvious thing I'm overlooking?"

Common sense is not as common as it should be. But when it shows up, it keeps us from wandering too far into foolishness.

Weather Around the Pillars

At first, I thought instinct, luck, and common sense were just decorative pieces on our metaphorical structure of pillars holding up wisdom. But they are not the structure at all. They are the weather around it: unpredictable, sometimes harsh, sometimes generous, always present. They remind us that no matter how carefully we construct our lives, we are never entirely in charge.

Closing Reflection

This book began with a road trip, a dog, and an unexpected lesson about slowing down. It ends with this reminder: wisdom is not something you finish, but something you practice, carry, and hand forward.

The pillars of experience, knowledge, and reflection form a structure strong enough to support wisdom. But the intangibles keep us honest. Wisdom won't guarantee a clear sky, but it will teach you how to walk through the rain without losing your way. Trust your instinct, accept your luck, and lean on common sense.

And when all else fails, follow Morrie's motto: stop and sniff everything (metaphorically, of course).

Knowledge may give us power. But wisdom is the compass that points us toward how to use it. And in the end, it doesn't always point north. Sometimes it directs us toward stillness, toward gratitude, toward noticing the ordinary.

Perhaps that's why this journey began where it did: in between a picnic table and a dog bowl. On that bench above a lake, watching Morrie pause mid-trail, nose deep in the air, I realized that what he brings to my life is precisely what wisdom requires: instinct, presence, and the desire to love every moment to its fullest. That moment on the hill became the seed of this book. And it remains the reminder of what wisdom truly is: not just what we know, but how we live.

EPILOGUE

"Wisdom is knowing what to do next.
Skill is knowing how to do it. Virtue is doing it."

— *David Starr Jordan**

In the previous chapter, it was determined that wisdom is often described as an arrival: an endpoint, the summit reached after a long climb through experience, knowledge, and reflection. Yet even at the highest points, one question quietly remains: What is it worth?

Not in money, or accolades, but in meaning. In the value of one life touching another.

The world seldom gives us easy measures for that. The moments that reveal what we truly value arrive without ceremony, and the choices that define us often look small at first — a single decision, made in the stillness of conscience, when no one can be sure how history will remember it.

**https://www.goodreads.com/author/quotes/223714.David_Starr_Jordan*

A Town Waiting for a Reason

In the spring of 1942, the mining town of Greenwood, British Columbia, was fading. The once-bustling smelter had gone cold, the storefronts were empty, and the mountain wind whistled through broken panes. War had taken the young, leaving behind the echo of what once was.

Then came a request: one that divided a nation.

Across coastal B.C., Japanese Canadians were being removed from their homes and sent inland under the War Measures Act. They were citizens, farmers, shopkeepers, and children: people whose only fault was ancestry. The federal government needed somewhere to send them.

Greenwood's mayor, W. E. McArthur Sr., received word that his declining town might be chosen. Some leaders refused outright; others hesitated, fearing backlash. McArthur paused, then did something unexpected: he called a town meeting.

Accounts differ in detail, but the essence endures. McArthur told the townspeople that the newcomers were not enemies but neighbours; families with nowhere else to go. Greenwood had empty homes, unused schools, and a chance to do something decent when decency had become rare. "We could give them shelter," he said. "Or we can turn away and let fear decide who we are."

When the vote was taken, only two opposed.

That spring, the first train arrived. The mayor and a small welcoming committee stood at the station. Mothers stepped down, clutching children's hands, men carried bundles of bedding, and elders bowed politely to strangers who smiled back uncertainly. Greenwood, a town on the edge of vanishing, found itself reborn by compassion.

Value in Action

McArthur's decision did not change national policy, but it changed the moral landscape of one corner of Canada.

The interned Japanese Canadians renovated abandoned buildings, reopened businesses, taught in schools, and brought life back to the streets. In time, Greenwood became a haven rather than a camp: the first internment site in the province, but also the first to greet its residents with dignity.

When the war ended, many left; some returned to the coast. Yet others stayed, married, and raised families. Their descendants still live there today. A memorial garden now grows in the valley, close to the river, raked gravel, stone lanterns, and trees that turn to fire each autumn. Several crayon drawings by the children of the area adorn the pavilion's walls. It honours those who endured, and the mayor who saw their worth before the rest of the country could.

He did more than open the town; he re-valued it. In treating others as human, he restored his community's own sense of humanity.

The Bridge Between Worth and Wisdom

That story lingers because it carries a truth larger than its time.

Wisdom is not only the ability to know what is right, but to act on that knowledge when it costs something. Value, in that sense, is the currency of wisdom: it is what gives knowledge and reflection their weight.

But there is another layer to the lesson, quieter and harder to name.

To recognize value in others, one must first believe in value itself, that human life, including one's own, is inherently worthy. McArthur could not have stood in that hall and spoken for compassion if he felt he or his town were worthless. His confidence in their capacity for goodness allowed him to appeal to it.

The same holds true for us. We cannot live wisely while secretly believing we have no worth. Without self-value, reflection turns harsh; knowledge becomes brittle; experience hardens into cynicism. Wisdom withers when it grows in soil stripped of dignity.

Self-value, then, is not vanity. It is the quiet assurance that we belong in the story of the world: that our presence, like Greenwood's memorial garden, has reason and beauty simply in being.

The Inner Ledger

Philosophers and psychologists have long noticed this link between wisdom and worth. Studies of *personal wisdom* show that those who act wisely are marked by self-acceptance and compassion: for others and for themselves. They are at peace with imperfection, able to forgive both error and effort. Their sense of value does not depend on applause.

It may be simplest to think of it as an inner ledger:

Experience records what we've done.

Knowledge tallies what we've learned.

Reflection reconciles the two.

But only value — the belief that our life is worth the accounting — makes the balance meaningful.

When people lose that, even wisdom becomes hollow: doing without believing, knowing without caring. Yet when they find it again, the simplest act gains moral gravity. A kind word carries the weight of conscience. A choice toward compassion shapes history in miniature.

The mayor of Greenwood likely never called himself wise. But his wisdom lay precisely there: in valuing people more than reputation, and worth more than fear.

Returning to Ourselves

Each of us faces that same decision in quieter ways. Not on a public stage, but in the private negotiations of worth that fill an ordinary day. When we choose whether to speak kindly to ourselves, to forgive an error, or to start again.

The paradox of self-value is that it is never fully earned and never truly lost. We rediscover it by reflection: the same process that transforms experience into wisdom. When we stop measuring ourselves only by productivity or approval, we make room for grace, and wisdom takes root there.

Self-value isn't the conclusion of wisdom; it's the soil in which wisdom grows.

It steadies us to stand with conviction, as McArthur did; it softens us to listen with empathy, as his townspeople learned; it grounds us to act with purpose when the world grows uncertain again.

What Remains

If *Beyond Experience* began as a journey from doing to knowing to wisdom, it ends here: in the quiet space where wisdom discovers its worth. Building on the idea from Chapter 10, we can add one final reflection:

Experience gives us moments.

Knowledge gives us meaning.

Reflection gives us understanding.

Wisdom shows us where and whether to use it.

Value *gives those understandings purpose.*

In the end, wisdom does not ask, *How much have you done?* It asks, *What did you hold to be worth doing?*

And perhaps that is the measure of a life: to plant something that endures beyond it.

I have visited the garden at Greenwood. It is tended by a dutiful caretaker, rooted in gratitude, and radiant each autumn with the colours of remembered courage.

Long after the speeches fade, what remains are the gardens we plant in one another's hearts.

Value, like wisdom, continues to grow after the work is done.

ABOUT THE AUTHOR

Steve Olson, EdD., spent the first 20 years of his career in the media, specifically in radio, followed by over 20 years working in education, and now, in retirement, he is giving back through his writing and speaking engagements. He considers all phases of his careers to be extensions of each other.

Steve was born in Calgary in the late 1950s and lived in both Calgary and Edmonton as a young child while his father looked for solid employment. His formative years were spent on a farm, where he learned responsibility, making it about others, and learning self-sufficiency. Steve has long felt that the training and responsibilities learned on the farm became the foundation for the rest of his life.

Steve's career started in radio, without the benefit of post-secondary schooling, as an announcer at 17. He says, "I didn't have the grades to get into post-Secondary, but I had 'the voice' and this big personality, and in those days, that's all you needed to get on the radio!"

Radio was an excellent career for Steve as he moved from announcer to music director and eventually to program director in a major market.

Steve's entry into post-secondary school came seven years after graduating from high school. At the suggestion of his then radio program director, and with his wife Libby's amazing and undying support, Steve was accepted into the Bachelor of Fine Arts (Drama) program at the University of Calgary. He worked full-time, went to school, and started a family. Learning to juggle multiple facets of a busy life became foundational to his success.

Steve's two degrees in drama (BFA, MA) and one in education (EdD) have been the genesis for many of the experiences in this book. As a post-secondary instructor, he taught radio, broadcast journalism, film, communications, and media studies. Significant learning experiences while dealing with students are also included in the stories in this book.

A participant in martial arts and cycling for the physical activity, woodturning and woodworking for life's mental and peaceful requirements, and home-made cheesemaking, sausage making, and sourdough bread making for the, well, just because! Steve has a greenhouse, berry, and fruit-bearing trees/bushes in his backyard. He still puts up jams, jellies, and a variety of other preserves every year.

Steve has been married to Libby since 1979. They have four adult children, many grandchildren, and Morrie the dog! After retiring, Steve and Libby bought a fifth-wheel RV and hit the road. They've been living and travelling full-time for over two years.

GET IN TOUCH

Website:

steveolsonbooks.com

E-mail address:

info@steveolsonbooks.com

Speaking Engagements:

Steve is available for speaking engagements by contacting Steve at: info@steveolsonbooks.com

He is also a professional Master of Ceremonies and would love to chat with you about your next event.